ANIMALS OF THE ARCTIC

Harp Seals

by Rebecca Pettiford

BELLWETHER MEDIA • MINNEAPOLIS, MN

Note to Librarians, Teachers, and Parents:

Blastoff! Readers are carefully developed by literacy experts and combine standards-based content with developmentally appropriate text.

Level 1 provides the most support through repetition of high-frequency words, light text, predictable sentence patterns, and strong visual support.

Level 2 offers early readers a bit more challenge through varied simple sentences, increased text load, and less repetition of high-frequency words.

Level 3 advances early-fluent readers toward fluency through increased text and concept load, less reliance on visuals, longer sentences, and more literary language.

Level 4 builds reading stamina by providing more text per page, increased use of punctuation, greater variation in sentence patterns, and increasingly challenging vocabulary.

Level 5 encourages children to move from "learning to read" to "reading to learn" by providing even more text, varied writing styles, and less familiar topics.

Whichever book is right for your reader, Blastoff! Readers are the perfect books to build confidence and encourage a love of reading that will last a lifetime!

This edition first published in 2019 by Bellwether Media, Inc.

Library of Congress Cataloging-in-Publication Data

Names: Pettiford, Rebecca, author.
Title: Harp Seals / by Rebecca Pettiford.
Description: Minneapolis, MN : Bellwether Media, Inc., 2019. |
    Series: Blastoff! Readers. Animals of the Arctic | Audience: Age 5-8. |
    Audience: K to Grade 3. | Includes bibliographical references and index.
Identifiers: LCCN 2018030993 (print) | LCCN 2018036176 (ebook) |
    ISBN 9781681036625 (ebook) | ISBN 9781626179370 (hardcover : alk. paper)
Subjects: LCSH: Harp seal--Juvenile literature. | Animals--Arctic regions--Juvenile literature.
Classification: LCC QL737.P64 (ebook) | LCC QL737.P64 P468 2019 (print) | DDC 599.79/29--dc23
LC record available at https://lccn.loc.gov/2018030993

Editor: Rebecca Sabelko   Designer: Jeffrey Kollock

Printed in the United States of America, North Mankato, MN

Table of Contents

Harp seals swim in the icy waters of the Arctic and North Atlantic Oceans.

4

They are built for the cold weather of this **biome**!

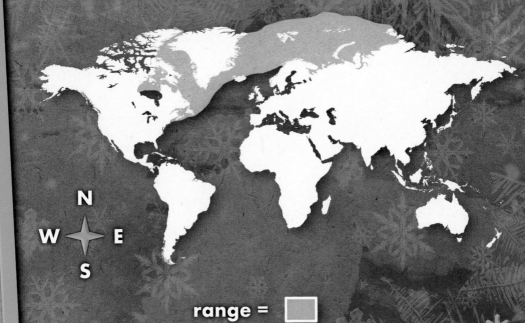

Harp Seal Range

N
W   E
S

range =

Harp seals have many **adaptations** that keep them warm in cold weather.

Thick **blubber** lies under their skin.
Oily fur keeps their skin dry.

molting

Harp seals **molt** each spring. Then, they grow new winter **coats**!

Fresh coats keep them safe in the cold wind and water.

Harp seals have powerful eyesight. Their big, round eyes are perfect for seeing in the ocean.

Special Adaptations

large eyes

strong flippers

oily fur

Their eyes make tears that protect from **saltwater**.

On the Move

Harp seals **migrate** south each winter when the Arctic Ocean gets too cold.

There, they have **pups** and feed. They return north for the summer.

pup

Diving Hunters

Harp seals are built for diving. Extra ribs and large lungs let them dive deep.

Sometimes, they dive
more than 328 feet
(100 meters) to find food!

Strong **flippers** help harp seals travel through water.

Their **whiskers** and eyesight help them find food as they dive.

whiskers

Harp Seal Stats

Least Concern	Near Threatened	Vulnerable	Endangered	Critically Endangered	Extinct in the Wild	Extinct

conservation status: least concern

life span: 20 to 30 years

flippers

17

These **carnivores** eat many kinds of fish. Special back teeth trap tiny fish.

Sharp front teeth cut
large fish into small pieces.

Harp Seal Diet

Arctic cod

krill

northern shortfin squid

Sometimes, food is hard to find in the Arctic. Harp seals can live off **energy** from their blubber.

These seals are perfect
Arctic animals!

Glossary

adaptations—changes an animal undergoes over a long period of time to fit where it lives

biome—a large area with certain plants, animals, and weather

blubber—the layer of body fat that helps cold water animals stay warm

carnivores—animals that only eat meat

coats—the hair or fur covering some animals

energy—the power to move and do things

flippers—wide, flat body parts that are used for swimming

migrate—to move from one place to another, often with the seasons

molt—to shed fur or skin for growth

pups—baby harp seals

saltwater—water that is salty; saltwater fills oceans and seas.

whiskers—long hairs growing near an animal's mouth

To Learn More

AT THE LIBRARY

King, Aven. *Harp Seals*. New York, N.Y.: PowerKids
Press, 2016.

McAllister, Ian, and Nicholas Read. *The Seal Garden*.
Victoria, B.C.: Orca Book Publishers, 2018.

Meinking, Mary. *The Dangerous Lives of Harp Seals*.
Mankato, Minn.: Child's World, 2018.

ON THE WEB

FACTSURFER

Factsurfer.com gives you
a safe, fun way to find
more information.

1. Go to www.factsurfer.com.

2. Enter "harp seals" into the search box.

3. Click the "Surf" button and select your book cover to
   see a list of related web sites.

Index

The images in this book are reproduced through the courtesy of: Dolores Harvey, front cover (harp seal), pp. 6-7, 8-9 (right), 11 (bubble), 23; Nature Picture Library/ Alamy, pp. 4-5; AleksandrN, p. 6; M. Watson/ Ardea.c/ AGEfotostock, pp. 8-9 (left); e-leet, pp. 10-11; Vladimir Melnik, pp. 11, 17 (bubble); FloridaStock, pp. 12-13 (left cutout); Michio Hoshino/Minden Pictures/ SuperStock, pp. 12-13, 16-17; M. Watsonantheo/ SuperStock, pp. 14-15; Doug Allan/ SuperStock, p. 15; Dave Black, p. 16; Dmitry Deshevykh/ Alamy, p.18; Vlada Photo, p. 19 (cod); Allexxandar, p. 19 (krill); FLPA/ SuperStock, p. 19 (squid); Roberta Olenick/ SuperStock, p. 20; Juniors Bildarchiv GMbH/ Alamy, pp. 20-21.